Understanding
FICTION

12

Understanding
FICTION

Poems, 1986–1996

Henry Taylor

Louisiana State University Press
Baton Rouge and London

1996

ica

96   5   4   3   2   1

Typeface: Bembo
Typesetter: Impressions Book and Journal Services, Inc.
Printer and binder: Thomson-Shore, Inc.

ISBN 0-8071-2110-x (cl: alk. paper)
ISBN 0-8071-2061-8 (p)

The paper in this book meets the guidelines for permanence and durability of the Committee on Production Guidelines for Book Longevity of the Council on Library Resources. ∞

Once Again, for Sarah

A Grace

I give thanks for the way our kitchen dance
takes on the familiarity of ritual,
from the moment of decision, reached
in a mixture of eagerness and relief—
you'll roast a chicken, maybe, or
walk us both toward boeuf carbonnade—
through the several sub-tasks
we can or cannot help each other do,
and we quiet down, hearing small
sounds of lettuce being torn,
prunes snipped in quarters,
the nearly silent bristles
of the mushroom brush—
and then the table set and served,
the centering on a moment of hope
and gratitude, as once again
we face each other, having done
a small and daily kind of work
in a large, eternal kind of joy.

CONTENTS

Three
FIVE OCCASIONS

Four
MASTER OF NONE

ACKNOWLEDGMENTS

Grateful acknowledgment is made to the editors of the following jour-
nals, in which the poems listed first appeared, sometimes in different
versions: *American:* "Centennial"; *The Beloit Poetry Journal:* "Unfolded
Maps"; *BlackWater Review:* "A Grace"; *Cosmos:* "Spontaneous
Generation"; *English Journal:* "In Another's Hands"; *Folio:* "Within a
Stone's Throw of Greatness," "A Voltage Spike"; *The Formalist:*
"Introduction to a Reading"; *Friends Journal:* "At a Quaker Wedding";
Mercersburg: "Reader in a High Place, Dreaming"; *The New Republic:*
"Afternoons with a Boomerang"; *New Virginia Review:* "Black-and-
White Photograph: Night Fisherman on Riverbank," "Frank Amos and
the Way Things Work," "Free Throw"; *The Plum Review:* "An Ending,"
"For Char Gardner, Preparing to Work Her Art"; *Poetry:* "Another
Postponement of Destruction," "For William Stafford," "Master of
None"; *Sewanee Review:* "Underpass," "Understanding Fiction"; *The
Southern California Anthology:* "Flying over Peoria"; *The Southern Review:*
"At South Fork Cemetery," "At the Grave of E. A. Robinson," "Popped
Balloon"; *The Texas Review:* "A Horseshoe to Hang Over the Door," "In
Memory of Brother Dave Gardner"; *Witness:* "Rawhide."

"After a Movie" first appeared in *Festival 88*, a collection of photo-
graphs and writings edited by George Garrett for the Virginia Festival of
American Film, Charlottesville, 1988. "Night Search for Lost Dog" first
appeared in *Elvis in Oz: New Stories and Poems from the Hollins Creative
Writing Program*, edited by Mary Flinn and George Garrett.
Charlottesville: University Press of Virginia, 1992.

"Master of None" was written for the induction of new members
into Phi Beta Kappa, State University of New York at Stony Brook,
May, 1987; "Afternoons with a Boomerang" was the Phi Beta Kappa
Poem at the College of William and Mary, December, 1992.

The author thanks the following people for assistance with the trans-
lations: Moshe Dor (Hebrew), Vadim Medish (Russian), and Krassimir
Kostov (Bulgarian). The translation of "Recruits" first appeared in
Crossing the River: Selected Poems Translated from the Hebrew, by Moshe Dor.

Edited by Seymour Mayne. Oakville, Ontario: Mosaic Press, 1989. The translation of "Good Friday" appeared originally in *Window on the Black Sea: Bulgarian Poetry in Translation*, edited by Richard Harteis in collaboration with William Meredith. Pittsburgh: Carnegie-Mellon University Press, 1992. The translations of the Kazantsev and Sokolov poems appeared first in *World Literature Today* (Winter, 1993).

The author is grateful to the National Endowment for the Arts for a creative writing fellowship under which this collection was begun.

– One –

UNDERSTANDING FICTION

UNDERSTANDING FICTION

What brings it to mind this time? The decal
from East Stroudsburg State in the window
ahead of me as traffic winds to the airport?

Maybe we pass the Stroudwater Landing apartments.
Whatever it is, you who are with me get to hear it
all over again: how once, just out of college

or maybe a year or two later, into the first
teaching job, some circumstance found me
in the home of an old friend, one of the mentors

to whom I owe what I am, on one of those days
when the airwaves are filled with football.
We remember it now as four games, and swear

to one another, and to others, that this
is what happened. In the second game,
as men unpiled from a crowded scramble,

a calm voice remarked that Mike Stroud
had been in on the tackle, and we told
ourselves that we had heard the same thing

in the first game. Odd. So we listened,
or claimed to be listening, and drank,
and took what we were pleased to call notice.

Never an isolating or identifying shot,
just these brief observations of crowds:
Mike Stroud was in all four games.

An astonishing trick, a terrific story—
some plot of the color commentators,
a tribute to a friend with a birthday,

or maybe just a joke on the world.
I tell it at least four times a year,
and each time it is longer ago.

Mike Stroud, if he ever played football,
does not do so now, but he might
even have played only one game

that late fall day in—oh, 1967, let's say.
We were drinking. God knows what we heard.
But I tell it again, and see how

to help you believe it, so I make
some adjustment of voice or detail,
and the story strides into the future.

FRANK AMOS AND
THE WAY THINGS WORK

My wife and I are standing in my sister's yard,
   talking to the man who built our house,
   across the field from here. He's retired now,

though he looks much as he did eight years ago,
   when horses grazed our hill. But he's not well;
   we've known for about a year. We ask him how it's going.

"Not too bad. They do this radiation"—
   he pronounces the first *a* short—"every two weeks,
   ten treatments. I've got these maps on my chest, see"—

he opens his shirt, and there the purple crosses
   and rectangles are. "Got 'em like that on my back, too.
   The lens that shoots the rays is up overhead,

and there's a big dish, like, underneath—maybe
   to catch the rays after they've gone through me,
   I don't know. The lens and dish are hung

to a big circular rack that they can rotate
   around the table, so you don't have to move
   when they want to shoot from the other side.

I told 'em today, my breast bone sticks out
   too much or something, I can't lie down too long
   on this hard table, so I'll just hold myself up

on my arms till you tell me I have to lie down
   and hold still. Seemed to go all right.
   I have to go all the way to Winchester

for the treatments—five minutes. Down here,
    all they have is a CAT scan. Seen one of those?
    You should. They run you through it and stop you

every inch or so, and it takes a picture
    just like you'd been sliced in two. Cross section."
    A grasshopper jumps against my leg; I think

of the day the inside framing got to where
    he could see how the walls would be, and he said,
    "God, this'll be a bitch of a drywall job."

He leans against the van, eyes bright, the last
    two letters of his CB handle—GRAYBEARD—
    emerging from behind him. "I don't know,

I just have a feeling, I think we're going
    to come out of this all right." We pass the evening
    talking over things you have to imagine

with your hands, taking turns with the pleasure
    of being understood, touching on work in the West
    Virginia coal mines, black blasting powder, the way

one man on a bridge-building crew would toss
    hot rivets with a pair of tongs and the man
    on the girder would catch them in this tin thing,

like a funnel, and then we get on carbide lanterns—
    back to the mines—and from there to the old-time
    gaslights fed by acetylene produced

in a carbide plant you built outside, just far
    enough from the house, because every so often
    a batch of carbide would explode, and you

didn't want anything like that in the cellar.
    Better to have it off a little ways.
    And all the time, part of me is watching him,

wondering how sick he is, thinking *This
    is the man who built our house.* Finally
    it's past suppertime, and he takes off.

We wish him the best, and send regards to Myrtle,
    and the old van backs into the turnaround
    and lurches toward the road. The rest of us

go inside to my sister's kitchen, and look out
    in time to see him coming back. He leans out his window.
    "Henry, I don't know why I didn't remember

till I got out to the road, but it's just come to me—
    the town lights over in Romney used to run
    on carbide, like we were talking about.

They had a big plant that put out enough gas
    to do all the streetlights. I just happened
    to remember that, and I thought you'd like to know."

FREE THROW

for David Schiller

Hunched at a desk, my back to a window
   through which, if I turned around, I could see
   fields I used to cross daily on horseback,

having scribbled some lines toward what turns out
   to be nothing, I tear off a sheet and crush it
   into a ball. As my hand closes, David,

I see you in the open door of a van
   at a horse show twenty-five years ago;
     you came five Greyhound hours to see me there.

You hold a damp rubdown sponge on your fingers,
   watching a bucket as if it might move
   from where it sits on the trampled ground

ten yards away. Your wrist flicks twice, like
   the head of a snake striking, your arm flows
   over your free hand, the sponge arcs and drops

where you look. You do this again and again;
   I retrieve, wring out, toss, and you shoot
   as you did our last year at boarding school:

as if nothing else mattered. I am the willing
   ball boy, knowing that this is how it is
   when my horse canters down to a triple-bar.

Those were the actions we lived in then. Now,
   I spot the wastebasket in living-room clutter,
   partly obscured by the leaf of a table,

and my unthinking fingers begin to heft
    this wad of paper. I still ride once in a while,
    and you, these days, are running marathons,

so things are mostly not bad. But much that I once
    intended to do shrinks now to this difficult,
    trivial shot that no one will see.

It needs a high loft to clear the table-leaf
    and drop straight down into the wastebasket.
    More touch than eye, you might say.

I watch empty air for the flight path, my hand
    flicks just out of my field of vision, thought stops,
    and one more time, friend, it falls in.

AN INSTANT ON
THE TIME LINE

Do you remember, memory inquires,
what you were doing when Kennedy was shot?
The catastrophe-hardened heart replies,
Which one? Not that it matters: neither scene
replays as clearly as the first time I saw
a twist-top taken from a bottle of beer.
It was in Roanoke. I came home from work
to find the Friday bunch already at it.
One of the revelers—I know his name,
but these days who knows what it's safe to tell?—
reached in the cooler and brought up a beer,
and smartly wrung the cap from the foamy lip.
I stopped and stared. He didn't look that strong.
Presidents and rock stars come and go,
and that picture doesn't fade. It wasn't much,
but I stood there on the surface of the world
feeling it as it made another turn.

FLYING OVER PEORIA

for Louis Simpson

The man beside me nudges my arm
and shrugs toward the window.
"Peoria," he says. I glance across him
at clouds and vague patches of earth.
"Where many things won't play,"
I say, trying to smile.

His head sinks into the seat back.
"I lived there for three years,"
he says, "thirty years ago."
He stares ahead; I don't know what to say.
It's none of my business.
"Funny," he goes on,
"but I've forgotten it, in a way.
I mean it's hard for me to believe
I lived there. *I Lived in Peoria*—
like a concept, you know?
Oh, I remember things,
little scenes, like snapshots.
God, I even remember the milkman's name,
and I only saw him once.
I had a job there, friends, a life,
and I don't remember what it was like.
My job took me away."

He won't say any more. He is
about to cry. Does he want to,
or is he trying not to?

At this point in too many poems,
I, whoever that might be,
would think of embracing him,
but it rarely happens. A man weeps
privately, another ponders
odd uses of a word like *concept*,
and below them the featureless landscape
keeps slipping farther away.

WITHIN A STONE'S THROW OF GREATNESS

Among the guests I talked to once
at a wedding in the late sixties—
back when the principals at such affairs
were my own friends, not my children's—
there was the father of the groom,
who turned out to be a vice-president
with the Hartford Insurance Company.
It had been almost thirteen years
since the death of Wallace Stevens,
but I put the question anyway.

"Yeah. Yeah, I knew Wally.
I even know why you're asking.
I'm aware that he wrote poetry.
I never read any of it,
but I'll tell you this:
he was a hell of an underwriter."

IN ANOTHER'S HANDS

When I came out of the hardware store
into the eight-space parking lot beside it,
a wholesaler's semi had backed into the drive
and maybe blocked me in. But maybe not.
I got in my truck and twisted to look out
toward the driver, who looked me over first,
then the space we had to work with. It could be done.
Her hand, palm up, began to close and open.
I eased the clutch, trusting only the hand
to tell me where I was. She watched the gap,
the truck rolled back, her fingers moved, then closed—
hold it!—and I stopped and shifted to pull away,
but paused and waved, wanting to hold a moment
when something, however little, worked just right.

ELEVATOR MUSIC

A tune with no more substance than the air,
performed on underwater instruments,
is proper to this short lift from the earth.
It hovers as we draw into ourselves
and turn our reverent eyes toward the lights
that count us to our various destinies.
We're all in this together, the song says,
and later we'll descend. The melody
is like a name we don't recall just now
that still keeps on insisting it is there.

AFTER A MOVIE

The last small credits fade
as house lights rise. Dazed in that radiant instant
of transition, you dwindle through the lobby
and out to curbside, pulling on a glove
with the decisive competence
of the scarred detective

or his quarry. Scanning
the rainlit street for taxicabs, you visualize,
without looking, your image in the window
of the jeweler's shop, where white hands hover
above the string of luminous pearls
on a faceless velvet bust.

Someone across the street
enters a bar, leaving behind a charged vacancy
in which you cut to the dim booth inside,
where you are seated, glancing at the door.
You lift an eyebrow, recognizing
the unnamed colleague

who will conspire with you
against whatever the volatile script provides. . . .
A cab pulls up. You stoop into the dark
and settle toward a version of yourself.
Your profile cruises past the city
on a home-drifting stream

through whose surface, sometimes,
you glimpse the life between the streambed and the ripples,
as, when your gestures are your own again,
your fingers lift a cup beyond whose rim
a room bursts into clarity
and light falls on all things.

NIGHT SEARCH FOR LOST DOG

Not yet midnight, but late, and in through the window
the sound of a fox barking often and not far away
made me sit up and strain for something else, a clue
to the disappearance, two days before, of a silly old dog;

maybe they were out there in some kind of standoff.
High whining under the odd crystalline barking
made me think she was caught on the fence through the woods.
So up, into clothes, the hickory walking stick Larry Higgins

whittled for me, and I went out into the late winter night,
the sky high overcast and giving back from somewhere
more light than I would have believed possible this time
of night and year, easy walking down the hill to the woods,

and there it was again, out the driveway and off
to the left, where I went then, onto gravel and clay
packed almost to pavement, not hard to walk quietly,
and the drive stretched along through the trees

as it seems to have done once in an old illustration
in a book my grandparents had. It was something like that,
since the sight of it made me stop and go soft at the center
that a landscape so long gone could still be there

under my feet, winding out to the clearing
where the fox barked again, just there where the drive
comes out of the trees. Quicker then, still quiet,
I took one step at a time, stopping once at a sound,

a faint rhythmic thumping that turned out, probably,
to be a wrinkle in the nylon parka working against

my own pulse beating somewhere inside it, so I went on
to the big field on the right, past the woods,

to the place in the fence where the barbed wire
will hold a climber with a stout stick to prop him,
and the fox galloped freely away over the hill.
After a while it was just myself standing there,

hearing for the first time the racket from the house
on the opposite hill, young hounds maybe sensing
someone walking and climbing as quietly as his age
and a noisy down parka would allow, but not knowing,

maybe, that he was looking for a dog who was born here
and stayed for eleven years, learning little, but loved,
then one day was simply not there. No sign of a fight
or the hoped-for standoff with the fox, or a coon,

rabid or not, the thought of which had prompted the stick
now supporting two folded hands, my chin resting on them,
my eyes going in and out of focus on a world that right then
it was good, after all, to be in, mystified though I was, and sad.

RAWHIDE

Forty-odd years ago in November, men
from my part of the world worked around
a wood fire with a caldron above it,
slaughtering hogs and a steer that they hung,
each in its turn, from a winch, to be scalded
or skinned, then gutted, bright shapes spilling out
just back of the knife into a galvanized tub.

On a whim, or to make an experiment,
the one man there who owned beasts and paid men
detached the penis from the Hereford steer
and tied a loop of baling twine to each end,
then hung it in the corncrib with scrap iron
dangling from it. In time it dried and cured,
stretched to a shape no one would recognize.

It was about the length of a good riding crop,
and he used it that way for a while,
then one day applied it, for a trifling misdeed,
to the backside of his eight-year-old son.
Thereafter, for some days or weeks, the hired men
derived brief amusement from asking the boy
what his father had swatted him with.

The boy, by then far enough along in school
to have picked up a handful of phrases
and a vague sense of which words to use when,
said, "Well, it was a steer's . . . middle leg."
Then the men laughed and looked at each other
from lined faces that carried old knowledge,
while the boy stood there learning the hard way.

A VOLTAGE SPIKE

In a motel at the wavering boundary between
countryside and a town whose name I don't bother to recall,
I stare through a generous window toward a clearing

of some half a dozen acres, bordered in pine
and a few varieties of bare deciduous trees,
the farther ones scraggling above a darker band

of background—trees even farther away, or a low hill.
Brown grass and broomsedge almost conceal the clay.
In the foreground a buried-cable pedestal rises

like a steel mullein stalk beside a walnut tree.
As I relax my gaze to a passive blur, the trees
darken and close in around a passing thought,

and the empty field becomes the backdrop
for a daydream not quite willed, as from the woods
come several dozen men in coveralls and stocking caps.

They carry clubs—of wood or metal, I can't be sure—
and move toward the center of the field.
With stolid care they set to killing one another:

the clubs rise and fall to a steady, thoughtful rhythm,
methodically cracking faces, bones, and skulls.
No one groans or shouts as the bodies drop;

even the sound of labored breathing is oddly faint.
I come to myself taking quick and shallow breaths,
my hands trying to crush the arms of the chair,

my eyes blinking to dissolve the savage tableau.
A light wind sways the broomsedge, and a flock
of starlings settles down like a cast of seeds.

AN ENDING

At opposite ends of many of their days
one of them tiptoed as the other slept,
since they were wedded to opposing ways
of keeping such appointments as they kept.
What came of all that care is hard to know;
gold foil and compass are quaint figures for
the wayward spirals of their to and fro.
They frayed beyond the grasp of metaphor,
but once at Coolbrook, letting landscapes pass,
he watched a ripple in the antique pane
divide a horse that cropped the orchard grass
beyond the post-and-rail along the lane.
The two halves stayed in step through edgeless air,
then joined and kept on grazing, unaware.

—*Two*—

FIVE TRANSLATIONS

WHO HAS BEEN EXALTED

by Vasily Kazantsev

—What person do they elevate
above the storm cloud's smoking wrath,
even above the stars, or fate?
—The one who brings the world the truth.

—And who is heartlessly consigned
to fog and darkness, in sackcloth
to freeze in mud and icy wind?
—The one who brings the world the truth.

from the Russian

THE SOUNDS

by Vasily Kazantsev

The woods resounded with a shriek,
a wild and terrifying cry,
but it subsided into stillness,
and I forgot it by and by.

In heaven's height a sudden flash,
then thunder rolled across the sky,
evaporated into silence,
and I forgot it by and by.

Into a wakeful midnight once
amidst recalled but silent speech
there made its way into my heart
the slightest ticking of a watch.

It was almost too faint to hear,
like a shifting sleeper's sigh;
I lay there staring through the dark
and seemed to hear it magnify.

Year after year has passed and gone—
departed, vanished, fled—
but still that feeble watch ticks on
like thunder
rolling
in my head.

from the Russian

RECRUITS

by Moshe Dor

Once I stood at attention among green recruits and heard
    the sergeant say,
"If any man here can translate from English, let him take
    one step forward."
I stepped forward. And was sent to clean sewers with my bare hands.
"The job suits intellectuals," the sergeant said, and laughed
    until he choked
when I dipped my hands in the gutter.

In the long years since, I have translated English poetry, fiction, even
essays on the Art of War, and still, I stand at attention,
an eternal recruit, a draftee forever. And when Sarge
asks his question, I still step forward smartly,
even though I know by now I will be sent again to clean
a gutter with my bare hands.

Conditioned reflex? Or a shining example to patriots?
Either way, the job suits intellectuals:
that choking laughter isn't the sergeant's anymore.
It's mine.

from the Hebrew

GOOD FRIDAY

by Kyril Kadiski

The streetcar, tired now, is heading home;
what's in our days, or in what we have done?
My neighbor in his kitchen eats alone—
Christ-like tableau, where no apostles come.

Innocent martyrs have died upon this day,
but which of them were what they seemed to be?
The thorny crowns that deck the naked tree
are empty nests; the birds have flown away.

Like beads of sweated blood, stars wink and fail;
the poplar holds a vinegar moon on high.
An aerial thrusts its arms into the sky—
a cross to which the living world is nailed.

from the Bulgarian

THE WRITING LIFE

by Vladimir Sokolov

To live in the love of a few, who never ask
that loyalty declare an outward pledge,
and in the gentle light of enclosing dusk
to lean to the tempting whiteness of the page.

Withdraw. Lose touch, let opportunity go,
renounce the world . . .
                      in this peculiar way
come to a vision of what none can know,
the future as plain before you as today.
A moment's glimpse!
                    and the prosaic rhyme
wakes to the kiss of genuine surprise,
as if from stiffened fingers, in wintertime,
the sharp scent of a crushed
                       spring bud could rise.

from the Russian

—*Three*—

FIVE OCCASIONS

FOR CHAR GARDNER, PREPARING TO WORK HER ART

As usual, keep your eyes prepared for things
you can lift out of their accustomed places
and assemble in conjunctions that show up
in dreams or momentary tricks of vision,
as when you round a bend on the interstate
and the passage of a distant hillside, viewed
through a narrow notch in the median trees,
has for a moment aspects of the whirlwind.
The weird shapes rocks on beaches sometimes take
might tug at some connection in your mind:
the realization that there are rocks at sea

can be like the discovery, once you learn
a language for the sake of its poetry,
that most who speak it have no use for poems.
Meanwhile your knowledge of your various crafts
constricts the boundary around these objects.
You try forgetting everything you know,
but some technique is bound to interrupt.
The shapes hang in your head like body parts,
and nag until you think of placing them
on a surface where they might cast shadows.
A plywood board. A pencil and a saw.

A shape that comes from somewhere. And then?
What next? The saw has scarred the board's edge,
which you may cover with a metal trim,
and maybe not. An hour of sanding helps you think,
or not think, really, as the shapes revolve
and settle into patterns on the board.

All this, you understand, is mere example.
You might be hoarding bits of twine or bark,
peeling the labels from antique tin cans,
or breeding chickens toward imagined plumage.
Somehow the ingredients will find you.

Prefer, let me suggest, at least one thing
that, so far, you have not used in your work,
whose behavior you cannot foresee precisely:
Will it crack or stay smooth as the surface dries?
Will it strain the joint to wet it one more time?
Preserve for as long as you can a mystery
about the way from one stage to the next.
What about added color? Or will your stones,
if that is what they are, want shades of gray?
At each step, fresh alternatives appear.
Some may find their places in variations

you make short notes toward trying later on.
Beware of dwelling too long on one phase
only because you like the way it feels;
even the most elaborate cuisines
require brief work with slime or shapelessness.
Some choices take too long, or cost too much,
so there are times when you settle for what will do.
But here, because you let your mind and hands
work as independently as they could,
you have the memory of what went into this,
and you are allowed to touch it. It is yours.

READER IN A HIGH
PLACE, DREAMING

for the dedication of Lenfest Hall,
Mercersburg Academy, May 14, 1993

High in a dormer niche that overlooks
a valley's gradual swerve from east to south,
a student holds a book, but stares away,

having just found a Latin adjective
that could mean either *deep* or *high*, depending;
the mind drifts in from mountain wanderings

only to wander on, down airy steps
past stacks of ordered spines, to lower floors
where, on illuminated terminals

at the ends of cables that traverse the world,
the world, or someone's version of it, shines.
Now eyelids and the book discreetly close.

The mind, set loose to move at will, drops in
on history teachers who convene to ponder
the valley's silent curve and how it speaks

of the nation's genesis. Someone points
to Rome, whose poet once let *altus* fall
into the stream of time that finds its way

to an oval table in a youthful dream
of abstract thought, in flames like a rare dessert,
served, shared, and savored till it has a name.

All these miracles occupy a space
that once was only air above a field:
brown lacewings hummed in sullen festivals

each spring, and Frisbees, launched in tilted light,
declined where now a footfall wakes the dreamer,
who lifts the book and thinks *lofty, profound,*

then sets to work where love and loyalty
have brought together steel and stonework, glass
and vision, in such constructions that these walls,

young students and their teachers, pure idea,
and grateful celebration all may rise
in unison from dreams of altitudes.

CENTENNIAL

*for the conclusion of the Centennial Campaign
at American University, March, 1994*

Men and women can put their names to laws
that live only in books, or a few heads,
while other names appear above the doors
to buildings where we test or break those laws,
becoming more of an idea than a place.

Think of a day on freshly leveled ground
when a dozen men in long coats and top hats
held plans for buildings in their hands, their faces
set forever on a photographic plate,
their minds astir with dreams of where we are.

For them the days passed as they do for us—
some like instants, others never ending—
while here and there along the string of years
they paused to make remark and tie a knot
to say that at this moment, here they were.

Today, assembled for another picture,
we touch the cord to hold time for a moment—
just long enough to let us say its name—
and give thanks for the generosities
that brought us here for love of human thought.

INTRODUCTION
TO A READING

Marilyn Hacker, American University,
March 1, 1989

First, *Presentation Piece.* It came along
when verse, hell-bent to be American,
was quiet, lowlier-than-thou, and slung
on structures no hip reader thought to scan.
Was the National Book Award a strain?
Toughly you pushed toward masteries more severe,
if mastery's more than writing like a man.
Wherever all those others are, you're here.

Between two continents, *entre deux langues,*
you found what lives you have to live, and when
grief, anger, lust, or joy rose on your tongue
you gave us *Separations, Taking Notice,* then
Assumptions, which should be in print again.
Most recently, your *Love, Death, and the Chan-*
ging of the Seasons, a long and stunning near-
novel mostly in sonnets, mostly clean.
Whatever else the others are, they're here.

Where are they now, Pope's "most," the knee-jerk throng
who, he assumed, could at least count to ten,
and might by numbers judge a poet's song?
Who cares? The rough and right? Women and men
who counted bars no bar to speaking plain
and shook their cages to refine our ear?
Let *nouveaux formalistes* fret and complain:
wherever all those others are, you're here.

"Boss of fixed forms," Marge Piercy said. No pain,
no gain or pleasure—the message comes through clear
in what you write and teach. Boss, let's begin:
wherever all those others are, you're here.

AT A QUAKER WEDDING

We have been schooled in silence in this place;
whatever words we frame to wish you well
dwindle toward the spirit in this air.
Now may my words and yours, our wishes, all
go spiraling inward to that center where
silence unites us all in light and peace.

—Four—

MASTER OF NONE

AT THE GRAVE OF
E. A. ROBINSON

Decades of vague intention drifted by
before I brought small thanks for your large voice—
a bunch of hothouse blooms and Queen Anne's lace
and four lines from "The Man Against the Sky."
My poems, whatever they do, will not repay
the debt they owe to yours, so I let pass
a swift half hour, watching the wind distress
the fringes of my fragile, doomed bouquet.

I beg your pardon, sir. You understood
what use there is in standing here like this,
speaking to one who hears as well as stone;
yet though no answer comes, it does me good
to sound aloud, above your resting place,
hard accents I will carry to my own.

AFTERNOONS WITH
A BOOMERANG

An insect afternoon
of annoyance, discontent, the vain wish to be
    far away, and I sit on the patio
    staring at lawn, woods, receding green patches
        with the impossible loveliness
            of vanished children's books—

        yet here it is around me,
consoling if not healing; I know no kinder place
    in which to bear involuntary gloom.
    Then across the patio comes a blur,
        red shorts, legs, arms, three strides to grass
            and I can focus now

        on Richard, coming out
from under the weight of his own troubles, his hand
    cocked, gripping a bright handmade boomerang
    that now he throws, like a knife at a target.
        For sixty instantaneous feet
            it flies straight, then yanks left

        and banks upward, tilting
into level flight, a spun, evanescent circle
    back to the house, then toward another sweep
    by the woods, flickering in and out of view
        against backgrounds of sycamore
            and maple, sky and grass—

a flutter of silence
to where he pirouettes, watching the cycle close
as the end of the spiral drops within reach
and he plucks it from air. Our separate woes
may not pass for more than a moment,
but this is the moment.

Not that he never misses:
the stick will spin too hard to be caught, or a stray
current of air from the woods grabs an edge,
or he has to look into the sun. Sometimes
the gravel driveway breaks his stride
over the dampening grass.

Twenty minutes, half an hour,
and his arm tires; still, it always feels like forever,
infinite small variations within
the aboriginal pattern, and I think
that whatever their use among hunters,
artists most deeply own

these physical mysteries
of getting a skill right, or nearly so, or, rarely,
of getting it wrong, the shout going up
at the botched release, the sharp smile of disgust
as the boomerang goes off course
and snags itself in a tree.

Error and correction,
flight and return, my son pulling hard as he can
toward making a life that is his, lifting

himself a little from his private griefs,
and me, for a while, out of mine—
and though the pain returns,

he gives, in fading light,
a look of birthright ease to a difficult thing.
Whatever unrolls on this spiral path,
lifelong though it may be, and hard, is worth no more,
in the end, than these crystal instants
of grace and lighthearted awe.

BLACK-AND-WHITE PHOTOGRAPH: NIGHT FISHERMAN ON RIVERBANK

The camera crops out all sound.
On the bridge to the fisherman's right,
a few headlights stammer between lamp poles

whose arc-lights, as if on wicks, burn
on the hard surface of the Potomac.
He might have been here forever, sitting

with his back to us, hands clasped over knees,
his expert equipment around him:
a handmade folding support for three

casting rods; a folding chair; a thermos
of coffee; a canvas pack; and, resting
on the pack, something that catches

enough light to hide behind. A radio?
Or is it only his patience we can't hear?
Lost newspaper scuffles over gray

cobblestones sloping down to the river,
and three lines slant out leftward
into dark. The fisherman's elbows

make dents in his thighs, and maybe a song
from a radio goes into his head, then out
along the lines of his gaze, over water.

SPONTANEOUS GENERATION

Van Helmont describes a method of producing mice.
                                          —*Pasteur, 1862*

Rigid, peruked, his head too large
for the body caught in an academic pose
before an undulant pile of rags and bran,
the wood-engraved biologist recedes
into the dog-eared catalog of errors
and corrections that have carried us this far.

Still, no one has seen fresh magazines
placed on the coffee table; on the dresser
plastic and paper shreds appear each morning,
and no one claims to know what brought them there.
The offspring of remembered purchases,
odd mutants darkly coil in dresser drawers.

Surround your putrefying house with gauze,
or seal it, boiling, in a vacuum jar,
then keep awake to see what life, what death,
ascends from nothingness to where you are.

AT SOUTH FORK
CEMETERY

It had no voice, or anything like that,
as it came across a field to where we stood
cleaning up an overgrown burial ground—
a quiet whirlwind we could see was there
by leaves it spiraled higher than the trees.

It slapped a leaf or two against our bodies,
then wandered on across the empty road.
As if the thoughtless world were generous,
we took that quirk of air as something given,
and turned to cutting brush and righting stones.

IN MEMORY OF
BROTHER DAVE GARDNER

I

But you know, friends—
blessed children of the all-encompassing spirituality—
good advice is where you find it. Yes!
I remember one time down in North Carolina—
well, it can't be helped, that's where I was—
standin on the edge of a sidewalk
lookin along that striped place,
peedestrian crossin, watchin for
that little round-headed dude up yonder
to turn from red to white—you know
he'd spent his life waitin to do that.
Course, them cats don't live
morn about forty-five seconds!
Anyhow, I turned to the lamppost
next to me, and there, about
shoulder height, I seen this little
bitty sign, said WALK WITH LIGHT.
There you go, beloved. Try that awhile
and see if you don't feel better.

II

You know these places where the road
narrows down, and they have it all torn up,
with barriers and cones and what-all
along the way, and fellows
leanin on shovels, lookin at you?
Down at the end, there's a sign
that says END CONSTRUCTION, and yes!

They ought to do that. Well,
it's a way of thinkin.
And at the start of pretty near
every one of these torn-up stretches,
they will have a big orange sign
that says BE PREPARED TO STOP.
Now, that is weird. I mean,
if you wasn't already prepared to stop,
beloved, you shouldn't have started.

ANOTHER POSTPONEMENT
OF DESTRUCTION

Banging out the kitchen door, I kicked
before I saw it a thick glass baking dish
I'd set outside for dogs the night before.
It skidded to the top step, teetered, tipped
into an undulating slide from step
to step, almost stopped halfway down, then lunged
on toward concrete, and I froze to watch it
splinter when it hit. Instead, it kissed
the concrete like a skipping stone, and rang
to rest in frost-stiffened grass. Retrieving it,
I suddenly felt my neck-cords letting go
of something like a mask of tragedy.
I washed the dish and put it in its place,
then launched myself into a rescued day.

A HORSESHOE TO HANG OVER THE DOOR

for Walt McDonald

Lifted one February from Maine
to early whiffs of a Texan spring,
I strolled with you on a brown-grass flat
and came on a horseshoe pitch where all
but one of the steel shoes lay cluttered
around the farther post. The straggler
at the near end belonged with the rest,
I thought, so stooped and hooked a finger
over it. I wish I could recall
exactly how it felt—fingertips
at the toe of the shoe, the moment
of forward loft, balk, and weightless heft
giving way to backswing and the toss.
All I remember now is the surge
of certainty, as cold metal left
my hand and hovered against the sky,
that the throw was good. It hit, bounced once
and clanged around the peg. "Ringer!"
you hollered. "I'll never play with you!"
Who knows for sure? We met on the downhill side,
friend, but too soon to say we're past
more jolts of pure, unreasonable good luck.

FOR WILLIAM STAFFORD

Someone we love, old friend, has telephoned
to let me know you're gone—and so you are.
I touch the steady books; my mind casts back,
then forth, and says, as you said once, *so long*—
I look toward seeing you everywhere.

30 August 1993

POPPED BALLOON

For two days, off and on, the little boy
inflated a balloon and let it go,
whooping as it careened with a Bronx cheer
to a corner of the room. Where, after a while,
he let it lie for another day or so.
Then found it, tried to blow it up, and stood
dead still when it exploded in his face.

He wept and banged his forehead with his hand
while I told him how balloons get old and tired
from all that getting fat and going thin.
No use explaining; he wanted to have it back.
There are others, I said. No, that one. More tears.
At last he huffed a desperate breath at it;
the air flapped loosely through the ragged end

and made a splattered moan like a ripped kazoo,
a ghastly, joyful noise that set him off
through the house again, amazed at what he'd found.
I cheered him on. How could I keep from thinking
of other things that weaken until they break,
and limp through the world, making their healing groans?
A few more breaths, and two decades are gone.

Now, here is this young man, becoming more
himself with every blessing, every wound.
Like any doting father, I have prayed,
but he already bears his share of scars,
and finds, in answer to my selfish hopes,
fresh uses for what's left of broken toys,
a keener ear for the joy in crippled songs.

UNDERPASS

We were walking at dusk through the neighborhood
where we had fallen in love.
Just past the theater, under the railroad bridge,
we paused to watch a camper-topped pickup
negotiate the dangerous clearance there. A passenger,
a woman of maybe twenty in close-fitting jeans
and the long hair of those days, danced down
from the running board into the street and stood
where she could watch the critical, diminishing space.
She waved the driver on, and as the cab
drew abreast of where we were, we saw
another young woman crouched over the wheel,
peering first at the underside of the bridge,
then at her friend or sister, and inching slowly forward.

They were young and beautiful, we thought. And so,
to tell the truth, were we. This was probably 1964.
We held our breath as they made it through,
the passenger floated back into her seat,
and the camper's taillights melted into the traffic.
For all we knew, they were taking it a few blocks,
but something told us they had far to go.
We loaded some dreams of our own into that truck
and gripped each other's arms as it pulled away.

Today, using the phone to do some serious work
on the miles between us, we thought of them
and wondered where they had gone, with what cargo.
Like us, they're pushing fifty, or have passed it,
and may, like us, have children on one road

or another. If we could tell them anything,
we would try to thank them for having carried
some fragile promises of ours to a place
where, as things have turned out, they could be kept.
Those decades back, my love, we wished them well,
and if that wish had any force at all
they came in off the road some time ago,
and may even be as beautiful as you.

UNFOLDED MAPS

I

Upstairs at the end of a narrow room,
the boy once had a bureau with a pair
of shallow top drawers. He pulled one out

and turned it over, and with red crayon
drew on the underside a box, and from the box
a dotted line along a stream beside

a tiny house with one red line of chimney-smoke
toward a stubbed tree with a hole in it.
There he thought to hide whatever it was.

II

Some days I travel more in time than space.
These faint blue lines are paths to where I rode
one summer, waiting for a horse to land

beyond the third fence of an in-and-out
and turn toward the water or the brush.
The course was charted on a posterboard

beside the entrance gate. I'd studied it,
but couldn't call it back for anything.
Some days I rode off course, and some days, on.

III

Even a topographic sheet could never
capture what it is to travel from
your collarbone elsewhere by way of points

of interest not to be denoted
on a dry table of conventions,
though "Legend" might be a title fetched

just far enough from where we started
to place above the story we tell now,
here beside this fire, which I mark *X*.

MASTER OF NONE

The plastic safety card
hangs from my hand unread as flight attendants launch
   their deadpan puppet show; like a motel room,
   this familiar strangeness soothes me into ease
   at being nowhere in particular, relief
      that it is too late now to make sure
         I am on the right plane.

   Out in the afternoon
at the taxiway's edge, men in hard hats are standing
   around a backhoe. The purpose of their ditch
   is invisible from here, but as it lengthens,
   I see myself standing as they do, watching
      hydraulic feet swing down and dig in
         to steady the machine,

   or the bucket pulling it forward,
as a man inches across a comic-strip desert.
   Like something alive, it changes the ground
   from which I will soon lift away; in the cab,
   a man with knowledge I have coveted
      sits touching controls and watching
         what hands can make happen.

   An old story comes back,
from wartime, when steel was scarce, and broken parts
   of farm machines had to be put back together;

on such an errand, once, my father stood around
for half a day, waiting his turn with a welder.
    To kill time, he wondered aloud
        how hard welding was,

        and the shop foreman said,
"That dumb son of a bitch out there learned to do it."
    So, out of necessity, he mastered it,
    and I watched him for years; now greed gnaws at me
    whenever I watch some close work well done
        and remember the shop foreman's line,
            or mysteries I absorbed

        from my life among horses,
who taught me, in their way, most of what I know now.
    With less faith, I have acted in plays, taken up
    trim carpentry, writing computer programs,
    tuning Volkswagens . . . these sidelines and others
        have drawn me toward mastery
            approached, or barely imagined.

        For the sake of odd skills
I have shirked the labors I live by, and pursued
    one more curiosity for my collection, or puttered
    awhile with an old one, thereby evading
    the higher, more difficult arts, such as knowing
        at sight the life-changing moment
            when the right touch or word

        might turn aside the rage
that careens through the house like electrical wind,

or when a hand, lightly placed on a child,
might wean him without force from the TV set
where, as long as the light of the world's last days
   washes over us, we can believe
      we will always be here.

    What more will I try
before turning again toward making what peace I can
  with the consequences of ignorant choices?
  What can I know now but ice clicking in plastic
  at thirty thousand feet? So I daydream
    of earth-moving competence, held in air
      by the skilled hands of strangers.